I0011947

Contents

A

Adobe Acrobat Reader

Acrobat Reader is software that allows you to view a PDF document (a document that can be seen but not changed). It can be downloaded free of charge from Adobe.

Adobe Acrobat Reader
Adobe
FREE- On the App Store

ADSL

Asymmetric digital subscriber line (ADSL) is a type of digital subscriber line (DSL) broadband technology that is used to connect to the Internet. It uses standard telephone lines to deliver high-speed data communications (up to 24 megabytes per second).

Analogue

Analogue is a conventional method of transmitting data. Standard landline telephones use analogue technology. It is distinct from digital technology, which provides for greater quality and speed of data transmission.

Assistive technology

Assistive technology refers to any software or hardware that acts to assist and improve the functional capabilities of people with disabilities. Examples include wheelchairs, prosthetics, voice-to-text technology and text-to-speech technology.

Attachment

An attachment is a document sent with an email message. Many types of files can be sent this way (e.g. Word documents, PDFs, Excel files, JPEGs). Be wary of attaching large files because these can take a lot of time for the recipient to download. If you have a large file, it is considered good practice to compress the file using software such as Winzip before attaching it.

B

Back-end

Back-end refers to the part of an application that performs an essential task not apparent to the user.

Backward compatible

If software is backward compatible, it is compatible with earlier (superseded) versions of the same software. For example, the Microsoft word-processing program Word 2010 can read files created in the 2003 version of the same program, so it is backward compatible.

Bandwidth

Bandwidth refers to the maximum amount of data that can travel a communications path in a given time, usually measured in seconds.

Bit

A bit (short for binary digit) is the smallest unit of measurement in computing. 8 bits make up 1 byte.

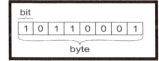

Bluetooth

Bluetooth is a wireless communications technology intended to replace cables. It allows short-range connections between two or more Bluetooth-compatible devices such as mobile phones, tablets, headsets or medical equipment.

Bookmark

A bookmark is a saved link to a particular Web page. Microsoft Internet Explorer denotes bookmarks as "favourites."

Boolean operators

Most search engines (e.g. Google) allow you to limit your search or make it more specific by using words such as "and", "or" and "not". These words are known as boolean operators because of their origin as terms in logic.

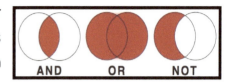

Boot (re-boot)

To boot (or re-boot) is to load and initialise the operating system on a computer. Think of it as starting up your computer. In Windows you can use the key combination CTRL and ALT and DEL as a "soft" boot. This means restarting the computer rather than turning it completely off and on again, which could cause damage to your computer's hard disk under some circumstances.

Bounce back

An email message that cannot be delivered and returns an error notification to the sender is said to "bounce back". If you receive such an error notification, check that you have typed the address correctly.

Broadband

Broadband is a type of communications technology whereby a single wire can carry more than one type of signal at once; for example, audio and video. Cable TV is one technology that uses broadband data transmission.

Browser

A software program that allows you to surf the web. Popular web browsers include Google Chrome, Mozilla Firefox, Microsoft Edge and Internet Explorer.

C

Cache

When you download (read) a web page, the data is "cached," meaning it is temporarily stored on your computer. The next time you want that page, instead of requesting the file from the web server, your web browser just accesses it from the cache, so the page loads quickly. The downside to this is that if the cached web page is often updated, you may miss the latest version. If you suspect that the web page you're seeing is not the latest version, use the "refresh" button on your browser.

CAD

Computer-aided design (CAD) is a type of software that allows users to create 2D and 3D design and modelling. CAD is used by architects, engineers, artists and other professionals to create precise technical drawings.

Chip

A chip is a microprocessor that performs many functions and calculations that make your computer run. Your computer's chip is also referred to as the CPU (Central Processing Unit) or the processor.

Cloud computing

Cloud computing refers to the storing and accessing of data and programs over the Internet instead of on another type of hard drive. Examples of Cloud services include iCloud, Google Cloud and Dropbox.

Compression

Compression is the reduction of the size of a file. Compressed files take up less memory and can be downloaded or sent over the Internet more quickly.

Content

Content refers to a website's text and information, as opposed to its design and structure.

Cookie

A piece of code or data created by a web server and stored on a user's computer. It is used to keep track of the user's usage patterns and preferences.

CPU

The central processing unit (CPU) is the brains behind your computer. The CPU is responsible for performing calculations and tasks that make programs work. The higher the speed of a CPU, the faster the CPU undertakes the calculations and tasks.

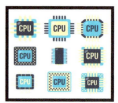

Cybercrime

Cybercrime is any type of illegal activity that is undertaken (or relies heavily) on a computer. There are thousands of types of cybercrime, including network intrusions, identity theft and the spreading of computer viruses.

Cybersecurity

Cybersecurity refers to measures designed to protect your computer, device or network from cybercrime. This involves preventing unintended and unauthorised access, change and damage.

D

Database

A database is a data structure that stores organized information. Most databases contain multiple tables, which may each include several different fields.

Device driver

A device driver is a small program that allows a peripheral device such as a printer or scanner to connect to your PC.

Domain

A domain is a set of computers on a network that are managed as a unit.

Download

Downloading is the method by which users access and save or "pull down" software or other files to their own computers from a remote computer via the Internet.

DV

DV stands for digital video.

E

Email

Email or electronic mail is a way of sending messages over the internet. Popular email programs include Outlook, Mozilla Thunderbird, Gmail and Yahoo Mail.

Encryption

Encryption is the process of converting electronic data to an unrecognisable or encrypted form, one that cannot be easily understood by unauthorised parties.

Ethernet

Ethernet is the most common way of connecting computers on a network with a wired connection. It is a type of local area network (LAN) technology, providing a simple interface for connecting multiple devices.

Encoding

Encoding is the process of converting data from one form to another. While "encoding" can be used as a verb, it is often used as a noun, and refers to a specific type of encoded data. There are several types of encoding, including image encoding, audio and video encoding, and character encoding.

F

Firewall

A firewall is a barrier that acts as a security system to protect trusted computer systems and networks from outside connections and untrusted networks, such as the Internet.

FTP

File transfer protocol (FTP) is a common method of transferring files via the internet from one host to another host.

Firmware

Firmware is a software program or set of instructions programmed on a hardware device. It provides the necessary instructions for how the device communicates with the other computer hardware.

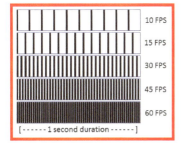

FPS

FPS stands for "Frames Per Second." It is used to measure frame rate – the number of consecutive full-screen images that are displayed each second. It is a common specification used in video capture and playback and is also used to measure video game performance.

Font

A font is a collection of characters with a similar design. These characters include lowercase and uppercase letters, numbers, punctuation marks, and symbols.

G

Gateway

A point within a network that interconnects with other networks.

GIF

Graphics interchange format (GIF) is a graphics file format. Because GIF files are compressed, they can be quickly and easily transmitted over a network. GIF is one of the main graphics formats on the Internet.

GUI

GUI stands for "Graphical User Interface" and is pronounced "gooey." It is a user interface that includes graphical elements, such as windows, icons and buttons.

GPS

GPS stands for "Global Positioning System." GPS is a satellite navigation system used to determine the ground position of an object.

GPU

GPU stands for "Graphics Processing Unit." A GPU is a processor designed to handle graphics operations. This includes both 2D and 3D calculations, though GPUs primarily excel at rendering 3D graphics.

H

Hard disk

The physical place where a computer stores information - applications and files - is known as its hard disk drive (HDD). The bigger the HDD, the more data it can store.

Home page

The page that an Internet browser first opens up to. It is usually the starting point of an organisation's or individual's website.

HTML

Hyper-text markup language (HTML) is a set of symbols inserted into files intended for display on the world wide web. The symbols tell web browsers how to display words and images - e.g. which colour, font and type size to use - and they direct it to link to other pages on the world wide web via hyperlinks.

Hyperlink

A hyperlink is a word, phrase, or image that you can click on to jump to a new document or a new section within the current document.

I

Internet

A set of interconnected networks that allow computers in different locations to exchange information. The Internet includes services such as the world wide web, electronic mail, file transfer protocol (FTP), chat and remote access to networks and computers.

ISP

An internet service provider (ISP) is a company that provides access to the Internet.

Intranet

An intranet is basically a private, internal internet specific to an organisation or group.

IP

An IP address, or simply an "IP," is a unique address that identifies a device on the Internet or a local network. It allows a system to be recognized by other systems connected via the Internet protocol.

J

Java

Java is a programming language that is commonly used in the development of client-server web applications.

JPEG

JPEG stands for Joint Photographic Experts Group, which was the committee that created the file format known as JPEG. The format is commonly used for photos displayed on the world wide web.

JavaScript

JavaScript is a programming language commonly used in web development. It is a client-side scripting language, which means the source code is processed by the client's web browser rather than on the web server. This means JavaScript functions can run after a web page has loaded without communicating with the server. For example, a JavaScript function may check a web form before it is submitted to make sure all the required fields have been filled out.

L

LAN

A local area network (LAN) is a system that connects computers and other devices that share a common communications line and wireless link, generally within a limited geographical area such as a home or office building.

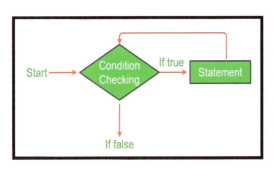

Loop

In computer science, a loop is a programming structure that repeats a sequence of instructions until a specific condition is met. Programmers use loops to cycle through values, add sums of numbers, repeat functions, and many other things.

LINUX

An open-source operating system that runs on a number of hardware platforms including PCs and Macintoshes. Linux is freely available over the Internet.

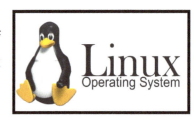

Login / Logon

The process of entering your username and password to gain access to a particular computer; for example, a mainframe, a network or secure server, or another system capable of resource sharing.

<u>M</u>

Malware

"Malware" is short for malicious software. It refers to a software program that has been developed to do harm to other computers. Types of malware include viruses, worms and spyware.

Megabyte

A measure of computer processor storage and real and virtual memory. A megabyte (Mb) is 2 to the 20th power bytes, or 1,048,576 bytes in decimal notation.

Megahertz

Megahertz is the unit used to measure the speed of a computer's processor (e.g. 2.8Ghz)

Modem

A modem is a device that allows computers to transmit information to each other via ordinary telephone lines.

Mainframe

A very large computer capable of supporting hundreds of users running a variety of different programs simultaneously. Often the distinction between small mainframes and minicomputers is vague and may depend on how the machine is marketed.

O

Online

If a computer (or computer user) is online, it is currently connected to a network or to the Internet. Online also refers to resources and services available on the Internet - e.g. online banking, online dictionary.

Operating system

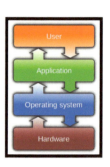

An operating system (OS) is the software that manages all of a computer's processes and allows programs and applications to run. The most prominent operating system is Microsoft Windows. Others include Mac OS X and Linux.

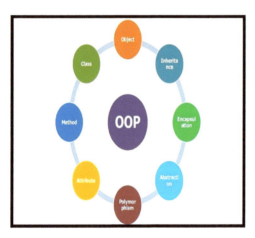

OOP

OOP stands for "Object-Oriented Programming." It refers to a programming methodology based on objects, instead of just functions and procedures. These objects are organized into classes, which allow individual objects to be grouped together. Most modern programming languages including Java, C/C++, and PHP, are object-oriented languages, and many older programming languages now have object-oriented versions.

P

PDF

Portable document format (PDF) is a file type created by Adobe Systems Inc. PDFs can be read using free software called Adobe Acrobat Reader or another PDF reader.

Phishing

Phishing is a type of email fraud in which the perpetrator sends out emails that appear to come from a legitimate service or reputable company, such as a bank or an email service provider. These emails aim to lure recipients to reveal confidential information that the perpetrator can use for their financial advantage - e.g. online banking log-in details and passwords.

Plug-in

A software plug-in is a component that adds to a software program's functionality.

POP

A Post office protocol (POP) is an Internet protocol used by your Internet service provider (ISP) to handle email. A POP account is an email account.

PPM

Pages per minute (PPM) generally refers to the speed of a printer.

Processor

The processor is the brains of your computer. It is responsible for performing calculations and tasks that make programs work. The faster the processor, the faster the computer works.

Protocol

A protocol is a standard or set of rules that computers and other devices use when communicating with one another.

Ping

A ping is a signal sent to a host that requests a response. It serves two primary purposes: (1) to check if the host is available and (2) to measure how long the response takes.

Proxy

It refers to a special kind of server that functions as an intermediate link between a client application (like a web browser) and a real server. The proxy server intercepts requests for information from the real server and whenever possible, fills the request. When it is unable to do so, the request is forwarded to the real server.

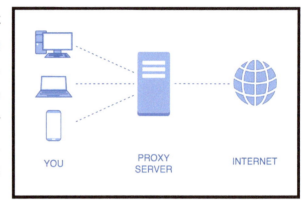

R

RAM

Random access memory (RAM) is usually referred to as a computer's "memory" - it stores information used by programs. Generally, the larger your computer's RAM, the more programs it can run at once without slowing down.

Read-only

A read-only file cannot be edited, modified or deleted.

Resolution

Resolution refers to the number of distinct pixels that make up the display on a computer monitor. It is denoted in DPI (dots per inch). The higher the resolution, the finer and smoother the images appear when displayed at a given size.

ROM

ROM stands for read-only memory. It is the part of a computer's memory that cannot be changed by a user. The contents of ROM remain even when the computer is turned off.

RGB

It stands for "Red Green Blue." RGB refers to three hues of light that can be mixed together to create different colors. Combining red, green, and blue light is the standard method of producing color images on screens, such as TVs, computer monitors, and smartphone screens.

S

SAAS

SAAS stands for software as a service. It is a software distribution model whereby software applications are centrally hosted and licensed on a subscription basis.

Search engine

A search engine enables a computer user to search information on the Internet. It is a type of software that creates indexes of databases or Internet sites based on the titles of files, keywords, or the full text of files. The most popular search engines are Google.com, Yahoo.com and Bing.com.

SSL

SSL, or secure sockets layer, is a protocol that allows Internet users to send encrypted messages across the Internet. It is generally used when transmitting confidential information (e.g. personal data or credit card details). A web address that begins with "https" indicates that an SSL connection is in use.

SEO

SEO, or search engine optimisation, is the practice of making adjustments to certain aspects of a website in an effort to improve its ranking on search engines.

Server

A server is a computer that handles requests for data, email, file transfers, and other network services from other computers.

Spam

Spam refers to unsolicited email messages sent for marketing purposes.

U

Unzip

To unzip a zip file is to extract and decompress compressed files from it. If you are sent a zip file via email, you will need to unzip it before you can access the files inside it.

URL

A URL (unique resource locator) or web address is the string of characters you type into a browser to access a particular website or other resource on the Internet (e.g. http://www.google.com).

UX

It means User Experience. Refers to the way a user interacts with a product. The term, coined by Apple guru Don Norman, was intended to apply to all products. In the tech sphere, it refers to designing technology in a way that focuses on creating an easy and intuitive experience for users. There are also customer experience (CX), customer interface (CI), and user interface (UI) in the same space as UX.

USB

It stands for "Universal Serial Bus." USB is the most common type of computer port used in today's computers. It can be used to connect keyboards, mice, game controllers, printers, scanners, digital cameras, and removable media drives, just to name a few.

V

Viral

If an online video, photo or article "goes viral", it experiences a sudden spike in popularity in a short period of time.

Virus

A virus is a piece of programming code inserted into other programming to cause damage. Viruses can be sent in many forms but are often transmitted via email messages that, when opened, may erase data or cause damage to your hard disk. Some viruses are able to enter your email system and send themselves to other people in your list of contacts.

VoIP

It stands for "Voice Over Internet Protocol," and is often pronounced "voip." VoIP is basically a telephone connection over the Internet. The data is sent digitally, using the Internet Protocol (IP) instead of analog telephone lines.

VPN

It means Virtual Private Networking; a means of securely accessing resources on a network by connecting to a remote access server through the Internet or other network.

W

WEP

Wired equivalent privacy (WEP) is a security protocol used in wi-fi networks. It is designed to provide a wireless local area network (LAN) with a level of security similar to that of a regular wired LAN. WEP-secured networks are usually protected by passwords.

Wi-Fi

Wi-Fi is a technology that allows computers and other devices to communicate via a wireless signal. Essentially, it means you can browse the internet without tripping over phone cords.

WPA

Wi-Fi protected access (WPA) is a security protocol used in wi-fi networks. It is an improvement on WEP because it offers greater protection through more sophisticated data encryption.

WIndows

Windows is a series of operating systems developed by Microsoft. Each version of Windows includes a graphical user interface, with a desktop that allows users to view files and folders in windows. For the past two decades, Windows has been the most widely used operating system for personal computers PCs.

Z

Zip

To zip files is to archive and compress them into one file of smaller size using a program such as WinZip. It's a handy way to make files smaller before sending them via email.

Zoom

The act of enlarging a portion of an onscreen image for fine detail work; most graphics programs have this capability.